m o o n
fev e r

Original texts and illustrations by
Véronique-Anne Epiter

© Copyright July 29, 2011

ISBN: 978-0615520513

Published by

Artiges Rose

Boston, Massachusetts

Boston, Massachusetts

USA

Acknowledgement

To **Rochelle O'Neal Thorpe**, *founder of* **Wiggles Press** *and publisher of enchanting storybooks for children around the world:*

Thank you for believing in this book and guiding me through the adventurous steps between its creation and publication; for your digital expertise, zeroing-in on my favorite color for its cover, and your encouragement to create my own label: "La Rose d'Artiges" (Artiges Rose), inspired by my mother.

Cover Illustration

The artist chose a whimsical ink drawing entitled "Pleine Lune"
(Full Moon) to illustrate the front cover of this book:

"I like the candid feeling of work in progress depicted in this
drawing. You have to look at it with a sense of humor, as it
represents the creative energy of the moon. The bold lines are
like the strokes of inspiration that this merciless muse sends
without notice, keeping the artist up with creative drive.
This is a vivid portrait of my new baby,
moon fever."

VAE

Introduction

moon fever *is a compilation of selected*
poems, thoughts and shorts stories
written over the past nineteen years.
I hope you will enjoy reading them.

This book is dedicated to
all my angels, down here
and beyond, with gratitude.

Véronique-Anne Epiter
July 2011

>>>>>Artist Contact<<<<<

Plume de Fleur Artist Gallery
Boston, Massachusetts USA

Telephone: (617) 227-7428
epiterveronique@gmail.com

Anchor

Love is more than visual
Entertainment or intellectual
Tickling
Love is something
Beyond
An undeniable bond
That sets the heart to pound
And the soul to rejoice
Love is a transcendence of sound
That commands the inner voice
Love started a long time ago
And will still be there tomorrow
Love is a breeze, an open door,
Love is the ultimate encore.

~ 2011

Between Us

Just knowing that you're my friend
Means so much to me
Someone else on the planet
We each relate to
Someone else with whom to share
The laughter and tears
And a hug in precious times
When there's no story to tell
Our spirits walk hand in hand
Mocking the years and distance
        Between you and me
Our spirits walk hand in hand
While ignoring the difference
        Between us and love.

Feb. 5, 1998 (Song)

Bead Work

There was a tiny bead
Of iridescent aqua color
That fell in the dirt
Lost out of sight
Purposeless –
What is a tiny bead
But another small link
When passed on a string?
There were many tiny beads
That had fallen along with it
Scattered on the ground
To disappear, buried by the
Elements and time -
What are the elements
But worms and slugs after the rain
Has beaten the ground and
Multiple particles of soil
Are being moved around and up
And down, incorporating the beads
Into the endless motion of not-so-still
Life? Other elements come into play,
Human steps and thrown cigarettes
And strolling dogs and playful birds
That will not eat the tiny beads.

I am the bead worker and day after day
Sitting at the same sacred spot under
The same dignified tree in the garden
Listening and responding to the birds
At play time, rest time,
Guessing who they are
At dawn and at dusk
Day after day I have retrieved
My tiny beads, one by one –
Extracting them from the dirt,
Scattered on the ground
As shining and purposeful as day one –
Like untouched.

What is the resiliency of the human spirit?
It is the transcendence of the madness in life,
That drops us deep down into the dirt
To be beaten and displaced by the elements –
Yet come back in full force
So tiny and so strong,
Untouched.
Every spirit falls one day.
Every spirit is worthy of being picked up
To fulfill its purpose.

The End

P.S. - I picked back up hundreds of these tiny beads and
pursued the making of my strings – small jewelry with a
spiritual meaning... Instead of returning daily to get the
beads back, I could have gone to the store to buy a pack
for a couple of dollars. I would have deprived myself from
discovering the joys of archaeology in my own garden.
Archaeology to me now means: beads on the string of
an artist's life.

July 2011

The Call

Walk through the curtain of your tears
Till you see the rainbow
Draw a bridge up across the field
To erase your sorrow
Your spirit and soul as a shield
And a guide to follow
Listen to your heart and shift gears
Now is time to let go

Breaching through the wall of your fears
Drop your arrows and bow
Leave behind the pain of the years
Plant a tree, watch it grow
Strong and tall and free, like a dream
Believe in tomorrow

Dance in the rain until it clears
And you'll feel the wind blow
Listen to your call in the breeze
Time to go with the flow

Like the leaf sailing on a stream
Time to go with the flow

April/May 2006
(Song)
To my Mother

Celebration

I stand instead of lying
I talk instead of hushing
I sing
Instead of crying
I am alive
Instead of sleeping
I share with you
The laughter
Because laughing is magic
Like dancing inside
I plant the past
To harvest the future
And together we can
Count the sprouts
Water the leaves
Gather and share the fruit.

Inspired by the Wampanoag Nation
- with Thanks To Robert and his Family

Connected to Painting
"Danse – Tu vas remonter aux sources"
(Dance – You will journey back to the source)
2011

Don't Try to Tame Love

I've held so much my emotion
from going in your direction...
It always seems that love for me
Is far away or long ago
non mutual or forbidden.
Out of your sight I kept hidden
my heart once more ready to go
and carefully called you "ami".
If life is fire and waters
My heart has cried flowing rivers
And longs for flying to the sun
But with burnt wings can only run.

You knocked at the door of my heart
and the inner voice asked: is this you?
You walked the secret path to my private thoughts
and the inner voice asked: who are you?
You said words of kindness that soothed my soul
and the inner voice whispered: angel...
You shared human doubts angers and fears
and the inner voice hushed.

The End of the World

Will you walk with me
To the end of the world
Will you walk through crowds and clouds
To the end of the world
Will you hold my hand through storms
To the end of the world
Will you walk with me
To the end of the world

Will you walk with me
Will you be my friend
Will you hold my hand
Will you walk with me

To the end of the world

2009 (Song)

Father

I know there's no man
Walking by my side
But every time I take a step
I'm walking on the palm
Of your Hand

And though there's no shoulder
To lay my head upon at night
Every time I sit on the train
I know that I'm sitting on your lap

Father if I believe
It's because you've been there for me
Hasn't Betsy always told me
To root myself in your love?

And if you're there
Will you listen to my prayer -
I'm praying for my sisters
I'm praying for my brothers
I'm praying for the children of the world
I'm praying for the children of the world...

2009 (Song)

From Above

My two tiny bundles of life
You're teaching me
What I never managed to learn:
Be and let go.
Somebody once said love is never
Having to say: "I am sorry".
Well, little ones inside of me
I have to say I am sorry
AND I love you!
I had no idea how precious
You are to me
Till I knew I might have
Lost you
And here I am...
My two tiny bundles of life
Have not left me
I am exhausted and happy
You stayed in your
Amphibious nest of paradise
Inside of me
Like two angels sent
From above
Dropping their wings
To be the sons of my future
You are the inner miracle
The moving truth
Bound to lead me
While bearing you
To a new land of deeper peace
A place for me to lean on life
Instead of irrationally
Stubbornly fighting against it
And build my faith in you with joy
You my little bundles of sun
You the Children of Tomorrow.

                                    1991

Grief

Grief is like mud it comes in thick layers
What do you do when you can't see through it
Feeling buried and heavily loaded
Can you still sprout through the dirt, take a peek
And know there's life waiting beyond your grief-
Can you stand up to the burdening foe
And against it become your own best friend?

Grief is like mud it takes many prayers
To build a heart that beats with no limit
A heart that flies beautifully mended
Free of all doubt and with an open beak
To sing a song filled with peaceful belief.
Please let my song clear your spirit of woe
And tell your soul that this is not the end.

2003/2011

I Am

I am like the branch of the tree
My leaves may fall,
But I will grow
     New ones

I am like the morning dew –
Cool legacy of the night
Dawn after dawn picking
The sun's first breath

I am like the fierce antelope –
Away from the hunter
Into the woods my shelter
Fast as a dart
     I will run

I am like the waves of the sea –
Following the dance of the moon
In tides drifting down
     And back up

I am like the elephant
Beyond time and distance
Never do I forget
     My love is eternal

2002
To my beloved Godfather
Lucien Edouard Epiter

In Mysterious Ways

What are you doing
Always on my mind
How is it out there
I know you never feel the cold
For every time I meet you
Sunshine burns my soul

Is it that something
About you so kind
That I cannot bear
Will I ever be so bold
To tell you that you're one
Of my favorite people
And even more

Love strikes
In mysterious ways
And that heart
I thought was mine
Is gone to you
Love likes
Just like a child to play
It took the heart
That once was mine
And gave it to you

1992 (Song)
Connected to Painting
"From my Heart to Yours – The Letter"

The Key

Sweet messenger in the rock
You came to remind me
That I am a Woman
But you wish to shield
All that makes you vulnerable
So you hide your kindness
Way out of sight
You disguise your sweetness
With all your might
Thus you can be unbearable
Tearing what we build
It's hard to be a Man...
I had brought you the Key
Fit for your heart to unlock

2008/10
Embraced Rhymes and Rhythm

Message

Remember your mother's tongue.
Cultivate the remembrance and expand it.
Search deep down for more words.
Do not allow anyone to stop you from talking
your Mother's tongue.
Write it down word by word.
Make a dictionary.
Every word you can't translate holds POWER.
The power of your culture. Of what prevails.
Of what is unique, because different. Original.
Fundamental differences are those that lead to
learning.
Ignorance is absence.
Indifference questions the beginning of knowledge.
Affirmation – presence of life that nothing shall make
quiver.
Be strong. Know yourself.
Let them know who you are – BE.

*With Tibet in my Heart - To all
Indigenous People of the World*

May 24, 2008

19

My Morning

On a morning the sun rose
Birds spread their wings
And began to sing
On a morning a child opened
His eyes to life
On a morning my heart on your heart
Cried all the tears of so many years
Without you

And that morning was a morning
Like every morning
But it was my morning
For you were here
By my side...

Undated Song
(Traveling into the future)

My Sunshine and Moonlight

My sunshine and moonlight
You are the ones I believe in
My sunshine and moonlight
You have your mother's heart

I can walk
on the roads
of the world
You never leave my mind
And sometimes
if it's cold
in the night
I close my eyes
to see your light
so bright inside

My sunshine and moonlight
My shining stars

~ 2009 (Song)
To Victor, to Willy

The naked truth

does not need

a dress rehearsal.

Once Upon A Time

Once upon a time
I touched the sun
In my beloved's hair
And burnt my fingers
Forever
Once upon a time
I bathed in the sea
Of his eyes
And was left with the thirst
Of meeting them again
Once upon a time
He took my hand
And I felt a wave inside
A marvelous wave
Of tenderness
We lay side by side
And both our minds
Were floating above us
The hard soil under us
Seemed to have become sand
Or feathers or clouds
And time had stopped,
Like the moon over the tree
And motionless we dared not
Even say a word
For our souls were whispering
Secrets to each other
And we were listening.

Connected to Ink Drawing
"Once Upon A Time"
(Il était une fois) - 1983

Our Story

All I want to do is dance with you
I know you always had it inside
Take me out to dance one night my dear
All I want to do is dance with you

All I want to do is dance with you
And there is nothing we need to hide
Take me out to dance without fear
All I want to do is dance with you

You can dress in white from head to toe
And look like the angel that I know
All I want to do is dance with you
And then you can turn the page on me

I will wear the dress you watched me sew
So I feel ready to take a bow
Take me out to dance one night my dear
All I want to do is dance with you

All I want to do
    Is dance with you
  And then we can close
    Our Story

2009 (Song)

Pep Talk

God is not our fairy Godmother.
God is like a busy nutty professor.
He can't do baby-sitting.
He has so much on his tray he needs
our assistance.
If we fail to assist we get lost.
But when we do the chores
He has in store for us,
we gain wisdom and
self-knowledge.
We earn the power to
lean on ourselves.

There is a thinking pattern that needs to be broken.
We believe in leaning on God, while the truth is that
he needs our assistance.
The ultimate professor has ultimate plans
and needs ultimate workers to help him
accomplish them. Are we up to the challenge?

Dec. 28, 2006

Prince Adam

My little prince in shining armor
I will forever miss your kisses-
"Bisous" and smootches
From your tiny lips
To my fingertips-
Your stories, winter and summer
In precious bubbles to decode
And how when I played my piano
You responded in your own mode
Playing your marbles in echo
My impromptu little drummer
You and I shared secret giggles
And with happy wiggles
Unconditionally
You always greeted me

Romantic prince in shining armor
Often lost in contemplation
Of your own shimmering reflection
In scales of coral, gold, honey
You adored the glamour
Of roses, so I chose
A white rose
To honor you on your journey

My valiant prince in shining armor
I know you will return some day
Maybe in your own disguised way
But I will recognize
The deep beauty of your eyes
For it is pure as your heart
And left in mine a dart

My charming prince in shining armor

2008/2011
A Tribute to Our Goldfish

Response to Lifestyles
and Language –

Sex is
A beautiful
And sacred
Act of intimacy
Between two people who
Commit to
Each other
Through love –
Thou shall not trash sex

2002

Short Story

- Hello, may I speak to God?
This is long distance...

- God is out of the office right now,
May I take a message?

- I'd rather talk to him in person.
Does he have a voice mail?

- Sure. Please redial our number
and I won't pick up this time.

- Thank you. May I ask who
I am talking to?

- This is his secretary.

- His secretary? Maybe
you can help me.
I'd like to know
if you have any openings.

-In what department?
See, we have plenty of openings -
but I need you to be more specific
and tell me what type of position
you're looking for.

- Well... I would like to sing.

- To sing? You don't have to apply
in Heaven for that.

2003

Sing

When the sky turns cold grey
And so do your eyes
When your soul wants to pray
And your body cries
Don't believe it's all gone
Hope, joy and sunshine
Don't think you are alone
Just look for a sign
If a song is flying
Then let your heart sing.

Nov. 2008 – Dedicated to
Miriam Makeba

The Spirit Still Blooms

Softly I passed my eyes over
The black diamond strings of your hair
What a surprise to discover
More beauty than my heart could bear
Your head was striped with snowy threads
Immaculate signs of wisdom
Bearing a change everyone dreads
With the majesty of freedom.

May 24, 2003
Connected to Drawing
"The Spirit Still Blooms"

Songs of the Inner Child

I am a child of the universe
The creator made me
Whole yet fragmented
He poured a drop
Of each nation's essence
In my blood stream
My soul is in evolution
My spirit a revolution

I am a silk worm
Do you understand ~
Yes it is my destiny
That I wrap my spirit out of sight
Into the cocoon of my songs
So that it may evolve
Through metamorphosis

I will sing for you
Turtles and doves
I was called to be your messenger
Whether you carry
Your homes on your back
Or fly from winter to summer
I will sing for you
Turtles and doves.

2007
To my Sisters

Spell

Am I under your spell
Or is it real

How could I ever tell
The way I feel

My heart rings like a bell
Trying to heal

I am here in this well
Bearing your seal

2009

Still Life

Can you hear the heartbeat
When it hushes its drum
And the forest is still
Under tears under sighs
Rain and wind have a way
Of embracing a day
Do you know that all trees
Have a memory?
Have you ever tasted
The clear silence of dawn
With the reminiscence
Of another dew kiss
On shivering petals
Wrapped in rainbow hues?
Till, clearer than crystal,
The sacred offering
Of a bird's first call
Awakens a new day.

2011
To my Father

Thoughts

Humans
We all and each
Do our true best
To the extent
Of our own
Individual
Limitations.
If we accept
That they exist
And bow to them
We build the cage
That holds us back
And prevents us
From evolving.
If we are blind
To the concept
Of mere impossibility
We hold the key
That sets us free
To simply be.

June 9, 2001

Thoughts

Motherhood is like walking on a string with no nest to catch you
underneath
Stretching yourself beyond the limit and having no right to pop
Storing in all the pain and storing in all the joy
And sharing the joy only but keeping the pain for growth purposes
Because being a mom is the most challenging growth path of all.

*

Clearly God meant to teach Adam and Eve a high lesson,
That he sent them parenthood –
The most alienating, long enduring,
Deeply, heavily challenging
Gift
of all.

Aug. 29, 2002
@ 1:25 a.m.

Through the Lines

I could walk with my eyes closed
Yet would still find you
When you talk time is paused
And I feel brand new

You can read through my tears
Stories in present and past tense
You can hear in my silence
Secrets hushed over the years

When you talk time is paused
And I feel brand new
I could walk with my eyes closed
Yet would still find you

Undated Song
(Traveling into the Future)

Timeless Cry

If I descended upon your homeland
Telling you I came to save you,
Protect you, offer you a hand,
Would you welcome me, hold me true?
Would you see me as a Father
If in lieu of honor to her golden years
All I gave your Mother
Were more sorrows and fears?

Would you bow to me with respect
If I broke in your home
Saying I have been sent
To look for a suspect
Then took your first-born son
So passionate, handsome,
Brave and intelligent
And threw him in prison?

Would you embrace my policy
If I violated your most sacred gift
From God who created us all
If I killed your daughter
So precious and so small
After stealing her innocence,
If generous and swift
I then made an offer –
An allowance for your silence-
Would you show me mercy,
Would you kiss my feet?

I should kneel when we meet
For no price could repay my due
And how could I answer your "Why?"
Even a stone would bleed and cry
Under all that was done to you
We shiver in the face of loss
How could we ever bear your cross?

2005/2007

37

Unconditional

Demonstrating unconditional self respect
is having ATTITUDE.

Demonstrating unconditional respect to others
is having a POSITIVE ATTITUDE.

To combine a positive attitude with attitude
is one effective way to cultivate inner and outer
PEACE.

12.27.2006
To Dr. Gerald Shklar

The Voice

When I do my share
God gives me ideas
Peace of heart
And clarity
Of purpose.

When I stretch the line
Towards willful destination
He points to the horizon
And blows trust
Into my sail.

When I rely upon
Silent stillness
The tiny voice inside
Suddenly full
Has its say.

2006
To Terro Nelson
whose wisdom transcends
time and space

Wild Silly Goose

Flying home is something I never take for granted. There is an ocean
between my life here and the childhood I left behind. So when I have
a chance to return and trace my steps, it is always a mystical journey.
I get teary the moment the plane lifts its wheels off the ground.
Instead of anxiously keeping my eyes open during the entire flight,
I learned to take a nap. That way, I am prepared to reunite with my
loved ones after a six hours leap into the future.

One summer a few years ago, Victor and Willy hopped on the plane
with me, ready for the adventure of the year. The staff on board was
lovely and gave them much attention.
-"Are you twins?" The answer came in one voice: "No," said Victor,
fiercely - "Yes," said Willy, cheerfully. The staff at once fell under the
charm of Victor's cartoon eyes and Willy's pearls of wit. This was the
start of a fun conversation, one of Willy's favorite activities. We were
flying flawlessly.

A few hours had passed. Willy was asleep with his head resting on my
shoulder. I felt safe and cozy with the wonderful, alleviating feeling of
going Home... "This is happiness" – "Yess!!" answered Victor. Everything
was falling in place magically. I liked the voice of the pilot, who had a
warm, humorous way to communicate with his flock - until he announced
a zone of turbulence and asked all passengers to be seated and fasten
their belts. Our smiling flight attendants strolled up and down the aisles
checking on everyone, then took a seat as well.

When the plane started shaking, we were all ready to be brave for a few
minutes. But things changed abruptly, the plane was leaping and leaping
as would a horse in a rodeo. I tried to pray and words refused to come.
The staff attendants were riveted to their seats and suddenly there was a
Hollywood quality to their reassuring smiles. Couples, old and young, held
on to each other, babies cried, people hugged, held hands, or frantically
grasped their arm-rests...

Fear dawned on me, for my own life and that of my sons... I said: "God, please, keep us safe, we want to see my family again." I gathered my thoughts and started praying for everybody on board. Only the movie star voice of our pilot kept a tone of calmness as he asked everyone: "Hang in there with me folks, we are going to be in this for quite a while..."

On my left, amazingly, Willy was still sleeping, with a peaceful smile on his face. On my right, Victor, ecstatic, was living the Dream. With each leap of our air vehicle, he lifted both arms up as would a happy, wild bird, with an expression of exaltation on his face: "WOOHOO! YESSS!! MORE!!! ONE MORE TIME, PLEASE!!!!" His voice loud and clear, his eyes shining like two black diamonds, he transcended the emotions of the entire plane – passengers and crew. The more desperately I begged him to be still, the more he tried to convince me that I, too, should be having the time of my life riding the sky! I was caught between intense fear and uncontrollable laughter.

This thriller went on for countless minutes. A few seconds here and then the plane glided smoothly, then again violent bumps were taking us up and down without mercy. Even the staff attendants had stopped smiling. Most passengers were numb with emotion, with the exception of babies - highly vocal but without an interpreter - and my wild silly goose with his clear, remarkable message. Victor knew, like our pilot, what the rest of us still had to learn – to keep an attitude of trust, joy and appreciation even through the utmost turbulence.

We landed safely, like in a movie. I had to wake up Willy, who had missed the action/suspense scene of the adventure. Our super hero Victor thanked the crew when we left: "It was the coolest flight ever! PEACE!"

The End

2011

Willy's Plastic Tarantula
and Other Priceless Stuff...

Have you ever vacuumed your kids' bedroom and ran into unforgettable treasures? Some of them, with legs... Others never to be mentioned on a college application nor at a job interview.

My son is a nature lover and, just like his mom, has deep respect for everything alive. However there is a certain creature I like to refer to as "your pet" that is inanimate, yet behaves in spirited ways. This manmade favorite of Willy's will appear in strategic spots at strategic moments. I go around the house looking for an extra quarter to finish drying my laundry, randomly inspecting every pocket in the process. I plunge my hand in Willy's evening gown and there is our eight-legged monster, loyally guarding my son's other treasures. I let out an operatic howl that would captivate the attention of the pickiest jury at any audition. Only my son, who had observed my maneuver, has a look of triumphant hilarity on his face. His secret agent really rocks.

I am going around vacuuming -my weekly hobby. Suddenly, something blocks the tube ending. I interrupt my activity to check the cause of this temporary malfunction. Guess! Here is the object of my fears again.

*This time, I call Willy: "Come get that thing, please." Willy
takes his time, he finds the situation highly entertaining.
I cannot, will not remove the spooky toy myself, but its
owner is savoring a "Raiders of the Lost Ark" moment.*

*Last but not least, we compete for the computer station –
so I find ways to check my E-mail when Willy and his brother
walk away from the desk, even momentarily. Swift and
enthusiastic, I descend upon the keyboard, only to find the
spine chilling, hairy-looking, territorial bug casually left on
the keys.*

*My father always says that the shortest jokes are the best,
so I will keep my story short. But the number of encounters
I had with the creepy crawler – on my pillow one night, in
the bathroom one day we had visitors (joy has to be shared)
should have contributed to toughen my skin. While I still have
developed no affinity with Willy's plastic tarantula, I have to
give this bug credit for its sense of humor. And I will do Willy
the favor to keep silent about his other priceless stuff.*

*The End
(for Now)*

2011

Wind and Waves

All you indigenous people of the World
Simply magnificent children
Of the earth and sun
You have inherited the majesty
Of your Creator
While you dance
To the wind and waves
Leaving your timeless mark
On rock, ice, sand, grass, soil
And while you sing
For the leaf and rain
Celebrating and giving thanks
For the fruit of the tree and the fruit
Of the sea and the fruit of the Womb
Before you close your eyes to rest
May you abundantly harvest
The fruit of your labor.

Your Hands Are Dancing on the Keys

Your hands are dancing on the keys
Of ivory and ebony
Like two birds of snow and fire
Their magic dance tells a story

Courage and grace through your fingers
Flow in contrast and harmony
Your hands are dancing on the keys
Of ivory and ebony

Fierce passion poured in lightning sounds
Compassion from a heart that pounds
In every chord and melody
Flow in contrast and harmony

Your hands are dancing on the keys
Their magic dance tells a story
As you climb higher and higher
In scales that lead you to your dreams

Keep shining my little big star
For your presence makes a difference
Your hands are dancing on the keys
Of ivory and ebony

True to yourself on your journey
You hold the keys to the future
Like two birds of snow and fire
Your hands are dancing on the keys

1992/2011 (Song)
To Liz

Table of Contents

About the Author

Véronique-Anne Epiter *is a singer and a self-taught artist. She started writing poems and a collection of illustrated children's tales at the age of 12. She and fellow poet Jean Iglesis co-published a book of poetry in France in 1983. That same year she left for the United States to study music in Boston, she thought, for six months... Not knowing that she would still be here 28 years later.*

Véronique's life was transformed by the birth of her children in 1991. They inspired her to create a large tapestry entitled "The Eggs of the Sun Bird," a project dedicated to the Children of the World - a theme that is always in her heart. In 1992, Véronique released a self-published book entitled "Poems and Songs," illustrated with original ink and pencil drawings.

moon fever *took her by surprise this summer - when she realized that 19 years had passed, it became her top priority. "I opened a couple of folders, and suddenly there were poems everywhere, it was a like a paper storm... I am very thankful to Victor and Willy for their patience and assistance during the creation of this book."*

Véronique's artistic expression is one that addresses all cultures, all faiths. "I write and sing to share stories, feelings, and positive messages. This is my contribution to Peace and healing in this world. I wish to bring people closure when they experience loss and grief, hope and courage when they face challenges. I see myself as a messenger, here to build a bridge between total strangers, to help them reconnect with their inner child and appreciate the beauty of Life."

Note to the Reader

A portion of the proceeds from this book will be donated to the Machao Orphanage Foundation in support of the work of Dr. Carolyn Rowley. For more information about the children you are helping through the purchase of ***moon fever****, you are invited to visit her website at: machaoorphanage.org*

CPSIA information can be obtained
at www.ICGtesting.com
Printed in the USA
BVOW06s1925260917
495979BV00012B/264/P